100 *Ways*
TO BE A
Chic Success
AND CREATE YOUR DREAM LIFE

FIONA FERRIS

Copyright © 2023 Fiona Ferris

All rights reserved.

ISBN: 9798869798442

Contents

100 Ways to be a Chic Success and Create Your Dream Life 7

50 Success Habits of the Chic, Go-Ahead Woman 75

To Finish 89

About the Author 93

Other books by Fiona Ferris 95

FIONA FERRIS

Dear lovely reader,

Are you ready to commit to your dream life? To live in a wonderfully positive way and receive all your heart's desires?

We might think we need to become a kick-ass go-getter who wears a padded shoulder lady-suit and carries a briefcase like when Phoebe from *Friends* became an executive businesswoman, but the truth is we can become any flavour of chic success that we like.

Maybe once upon a time I thought of success as a fancy job where I got to dress up each day, but I have since found out that *my* happy place is to write books in my cozy little home office in the country (but still only be five minutes' drive from town), and live a simple and peaceful life with lots of free time and space around me.

That's *my* idea of a dream lifestyle; your version might be completely different. You might like to travel lots. Be right in the city. Or live in a big, beautifully messy, noisy house full of children.

We all get to choose our ideal life! And that's what this mini-book is all about. One-hundred inspiring ways to create *your* version of a chic and successful life. It's so fun to think about and dream up how that life could look.

But I get it, we can forget that we even have the power to choose, when we are busy at work, it's cold and rainy outside, the traffic is bad, and we don't have any groceries in the house because we ran out of time to go to the supermarket. At those times it's hard to remember to lift our head up and actually dream.

At the risk of sounding completely cliched, *we only get one life*. And, it's ticking away by the second. We can't press Pause and have it wait for us.

So instead, why not have a little fun with it? Make it sparkly and happy and enjoyable every day? It's available for us, and *all we have to do is ask*. We just have to remember what we want and then start doing all those things towards our idealistic, pretty picture.

I hope you receive bucketloads of inspiration from this book to find out and create *your* happy place. I know you can bring your dream lifestyle into reality, and more importantly I hope *you* know you can do it. Your wonderfully inspiring daily happiness is out there and it's waiting for you to make a decision. A decision that *you* are going to live the life of your dreams, however those dreams are shaped.

Exciting times! Now let's get straight into one-hundred ways to be a chic success and start creating *your* dream life. It's full immersion, baby, just dive on in.

I hope you have fun!

Fiona

100 Ways to be a Chic Success and Create Your Dream Life

1. **Conjure up the most perfect lifestyle you can imagine.** Make it amazing and note down all the magical details. Consider the sky to be the limit and that there is no cap on what you can be, have or do. I decided that I wanted to spend most of my time at home, doing something creative and feeling like I am on vacation every day. I wanted our home to have the ambience of a relaxing and inspiring resort. The desire to live a slower, simpler life is why my husband and I decided to move out of the city to a smaller area called Hawke's Bay, which is where I grew up. It's a sunny wine region with its own micro-climate. Because property is less expensive here, we could

afford a nicer home on land. I had the resort-style vibe in mind, and our home even came with its own palm trees. This fun little detail really blew my mind with its perfectness!

2. **Start doing things that are fun for you**. I decided to write about what made *me* happy; it didn't matter if anyone reading thought I was flossy, flowery, or airy-fairy (like those are bad things!) If it made me happy, it belonged on my blog and in my books. I also play around with my style files and inspire myself with curated magazine pages and self-written inspiration in my journals, where I go to dream about pretty things, personal development, and my own chic and feminine goals. And I create with my hands too – sewing, knitting and other handcrafts. Not everything all of the time of course, but I make sure there is at least a little time for enjoyable pursuits every single day.

3. **Don't worry about the opinions of others**. If you are drawn towards something, that's enough. And don't try to change anyone else's mind about anything either. Just make your own fun and whoever wants to join you will join you. The surest way to a mediocre life is to spend time wondering what others will think of you. Don't do it! Dream up a life that makes your heart go pitter-patter and start

moving towards it every day. Follow your dreams before you can talk yourself out of them, because sometimes your 'Let's be sensible' voice pipes up (and she is very stifling). Be someone who shoots for the stars. You might not carry every plan out, but at least write them all down in your 'amazing dream life' notebook because *you never know*.

4. **Be creative every day**. Don't save your creativity for special occasions because it will wither up and die! Inspire yourself *every day* with your favourite form of creativity – writing, baking, photography, art, music, gardening, home décor, painting, sewing, journalling etc. Ask yourself what you loved to do as a child if you've forgotten, and start doing that thing again. Lift yourself up and make your life a symphony with the way you live it. Swap screen time for creative time even if only for a short while each day to begin with. The more you do it, the easier it will get, and the more you will *want* to be creative.

5. **Clear the obstacles between you and your dream life**. Make decluttering a regular part of your existence. I always feel freer and more positive when I've let things go: items that are part of my old life, not the new vision for my future that I am constantly creating. I'm not saying you need to get rid of everything,

just the things that feel staid and like they are pulling you back. The clothing/ furniture/ décor items that feel authentically *you* whether you've had them for five minutes or twenty years; those are the keepers. Curate your life regularly and move forward feeling light and hopeful.

6. **Share your dreams and aspirations with your other half**. It is human nature to want to improve ourselves. Just like in nature, if we're not growing we're dying. Trees never stay the same. They are always growing bigger, getting more leaves, and expanding. Decide that you get to be the keeper of the dreams in your relationship (and if you are single, be it for yourself). Be the light who shines on your dreams. Talk of scenarios such as 'Imagine if we could live like this every day' when you are sitting outside in the sun at a café. Remember that cheesy saying: 'Teamwork makes the dream work'. Dream big dreams for the both of you. When you do this, magic is set into motion. Want more. Have big desires.

7. **Be inspired by others' successes** and know that you can do the same if you want to. Sure, some people might have advantages that normal people like you and I don't, but don't let that stop you from being motivated by what they have achieved. You can still do things in

your own way *and* be a big success in the way you live your life. Find mentors who inspire you and top up on their inspiration often. My mentors are mostly online, covering the areas of living a simple life, self-development, and creating a fabulous personal style. They help me build a wonderful future and I am so grateful! What are the topics you are most passionate about and how can you learn from and be inspired by others?

8. **Change habits effortlessly with your 'dream life' goals.** Goal setting will get you your dream life and more, but in many different ways than you would think. As you choose goals for the month, week, or season and refocus on them daily, habits that you had tried to stop previously will simply dissolve without effort. For me that meant online shopping, nibbling on sweet treats, and sipping brandy at night with a bowl of potato chips. They were always in the background beckoning to me. But when I became excited about my goals, dreams, and projects, focusing on a few at a time, that became much more fun to me. Amazingly I simply 'forgot' about those other activities that used to give me pleasure (but also 'pain' in the form of money spent or weight gain!)

9. **Be inspired by your future self**. Picture yourself ten years into the future and really study who you have become. See your beautiful home where you now live. Look at your fit and healthy physique. You no longer have to worry about finding your purpose. You no longer have to obsess over every single cent that you spend. You realize that you are living your dream life. Now ask the future you how she got there. What kinds of things did she do? What did she start believing is possible? When I have had fun little journal sessions asking myself these sorts of questions I have gained fabulous insights and ideas to try that I wouldn't have come up with 'on my own'. Ask your future self for encouragement and inspiration; she is waiting for you!

10. **Don't be average and your life won't be average**. I heard this phrase on a YouTube video and it stuck with me because it's so simple and so good! Be willing to do things that others are not willing to do. Remember your dreams and goals every day and *do something towards them* even if it's tiny. Commit to achieving your goals and do whatever it takes to get there. Disregard naysayers, procrastination, your own self-limiting beliefs, doubts, fear, worry, perceived lack of time, not being good enough and all those 'reasons' why you should just quit and be

'normal'. It doesn't have to be a hard slog either. Make it fun and exciting. Dream of how good things are going to be. You'll be jumping out of bed in the morning, I promise.

11. **Expect to still be the same lovely person.** Phew! Know that you don't have to become someone different to become a chic success. You may be richer, fitter, more focused and excited to do big things, but you are still the same kind, caring, sweet person. And also, you're not. Here's what I mean. You have kept all the good parts of yourself but replaced the self-sabotaging, doubting parts – with confidence, excitement, and enthusiasm for your new direction. Whether that direction is getting in kick-ass shape, writing a book, starting your own business, starting a family, or pivoting in your career. It will look to others as if you have a new lease of life, because... you have!

12. **Be someone who sets and achieves goals** by taking small steps towards those goals every day. Eat the elephant one bite at a time and feel *so* proud of yourself when you look back at how far you have come in one, two, or three months' time and one, two, or three years' time. When you set a goal initially, brainstorm a long, delicious list of all the little steps, tips, ways, ideas, and helpful hints on how you can

get there. Then add to it with online searches of the same. Make this list so exciting and compelling that you can't help but be motivated by it. And read it every day! You will find you don't need to push yourself because it will be so exciting to do all these little things towards your goals.

13. **Remember your desires daily**. When you want to really move ahead quickly with a goal, such as saving up for a home improvement project or creating a healthier lifestyle, remind yourself *every day* of what you want. What this could look like is writing twice a day – in the morning and before you go to bed – in your journal. Give yourself a pep-talk, write a page full of 'I am...' statements, or envisage how wonderful it's going to be when you reach that dream goal. Write everything in the present tense and keep your desires top of mind. If you are not a journal person maybe you'll have sticky notes up around the place to remind you. Or create a vision board with pictures. A journal full of inspiring words is *my* favourite way, and Pinterest boards online a close second. The most important thing is that you remember your desires, daily.

14. **Keep on going even when the excitement wears off**. Not every day can be a fireworks display of enthusiasm. Your initial excitement for your goal will start to wear off at some stage. The inspiration you had at the beginning will no longer do it for you. That's when you have to accept that it may be a long journey. But that's okay, you have the rest of your life to get there. And are you willing to give up on your dreams? That goal you set for yourself whether it's to lose weight, pay off debt, or complete your degree? No! You are there for yourself. You are committed to your future. And all you have to do is remember what you want. Keep that picture in front of you all the time. Find new inspiration to keep you going, to keep fanning the flames. Go slower to go faster, which means if you keep on going, you will eventually get there. Don't stop and start if it doesn't happen instantly. You are in this for the long haul!

15. **Replace news with inspiration**. I have deleted the news apps from my phone more times than I can count. I did it initially so the news wouldn't be the first place I'd go to when I wanted a quiet five minutes to play with my phone. Invariably I'd end up depressed, grumpy, or both at once. But when I deleted the three news apps I had, a vacuum opened up. What would I look at? My two new choices

were the Kindle app, for a quick dip into an inspiring non-fiction book, or my Pinterest boards, also inspiring! Both give me a five-minute pep talk or boost of inspiration and it's wonderful. Whenever I have reloaded a news app 'to keep in touch' or because 'they might have changed', I have always regretted it. If you don't need that kind of drain on your happiness, consider cleansing your phone of malignant apps too. It doesn't need to be just news either; if an app makes you feel sad, unhappy or 'less than', it needs to go.

16. **Find the lazy way.** While I am a big fan of setting goals and creating a successful life for myself in all areas, I'm *not* so keen on hard work, knuckling down or even worse, depriving myself. That's why I always like to ask, 'How can I make this fun and easy?' It's probably one of the most used questions in my journal. For some hormonal weight gain I've had lately, I asked myself this question and created a wonderfully long list, none of which involved cutting carbs, counting calories or intermittent fasting. In my list a few points jumped out for me: namely to halve my meal size (my portions had gotten too big), journal pep talks for myself each morning, and read Kindle books or listen to YouTube videos on the subject of weight loss to gain inspiration and new ideas. Incredibly, doing these things

helped me not wants snacks and sweets, so the only 'job' I had was to make my meals smaller and this was easy – I was still full afterwards. So you can see that finding the lazy way is actually really smart, not lazy! What goal of *yours* would you like to transform?

17. **Elevate your standards**. Where in your life are your standards slipping? Where are you letting yourself down? Look at yourself objectively and go through each category in your life as an impartial consultant. When we first moved into our current home it was huge compared to our previous home, and we simply didn't have enough furniture to fill it. I ended up becoming friendly with a local interior designer whom we bought some pieces through, and she helped me realise our vision. I remember I was showing her my dining suite options, and she said of them, 'You can do better'. Now, better to her was not necessarily spending more. Her advice was to go to an auction house and buy a vintage table and chairs versus paying full retail for a lower-quality suite. We did exactly that and it worked out perfectly, and since then, I've often used her phrase when I am contemplating settling for 'normal', not 'wow'. Because why choose mediocre when sparkling is on offer?

18. **Design a goal pyramid.** I was listening to a motivational YouTube video the other day while I put my makeup on, and the speaker mentioned a goal pyramid. Whaaaaat? I'd never heard of such a thing, so I immediately paused the video and looked it up. Such fun! There are tons of goal pyramid templates online, some blank and some filled in with different goals such as weight loss. As far as I can tell, you list your ultimate goal: 'In X amount of time I will achieve this' at the top of the pyramid (perhaps, 'I will have written a book!'), then the next section down is monthly goals ('I complete my first draft'), then weekly goals below that ('I complete two chapters'), then daily ('I write 500 words a day'). You get the point, right? It's basically breaking a big goal down into smaller, more palatable chunks, but made fun with a drawing. If you're like me and all about whatever it takes to enthuse yourself, why not try a goal pyramid? If nothing else, it's an inspiring visual to motivate yourself, with fun little boxes to fill in!

19. **List one-hundred benefits.** No matter your goal, create your own fire by listing at least one-hundred benefits to reaching it – or even two-hundred! List *all* the reasons why you would want this thing, why it would be amazing, what you would gain from it, and all

the fun and fabulous benefits you would receive by reaching it. You are creating your own list of 'whys', and the more details you can add into your list, the easier it will be for any self-sabotaging habits to cease without effort. It's almost a magical process. When you are focusing on how great it will be when you get there, you are *not* thinking how *hard* it's going to be or what you will have to give up. It will be 'Game on!' and you'll find yourself raring to go. I've done this, and it totally works. Plus, in times when I temporarily 'forgot' that I even wanted this thing in the first place (it happens!), I read my list to rekindle my flame all over again.

20. **Look upon any day as the perfect day to start a new goal**. Instead of waiting until the New Year, or Monday, or the first day of the month to start something new, start today, right now! I love starting a healthy eating regime on a Friday, or a decluttering project two weeks before Christmas. Whenever the idea strikes you, or you receive a hit of inspiration from someone else, start right then and there. You will ride that mini-wave of momentum and get your goal off the ground really quickly. Plus, it will be fun. If you park it in your planner for Monday, your enthusiasm will have worn off and you won't even want to do it anymore. I promise you this is true from

personal experience. So don't worry if it's not what other people do, be different. Do what *you* do.

21. **Create an ever-growing stash of success thoughts for yourself.** I have a file called 'Fiona's Success Thoughts' on my computer, and it's a long list of affirmations I have added to over time. It's fabulous! I am continually inspired while I am writing it, and also when I re-read and add to it. I tell myself: *I make things happen. I keep on top of my admin and love seeing my desk clean and tidy. I find being organized enjoyable. My life and business is allowed to be easy and fun. I am successful because I do what other people are not willing to do. I live like no-one else today so I can live like no-one else tomorrow* (thanks Dave Ramsey for that one!). I'm telling you, writing a list like this for yourself and reading through it will light a fire under you. You will be encouraged to follow your dreams, trust in your goals, and know that they will happen. No matter your goal, having a motivating list of success thoughts will help you get there!

22. **Ask yourself 'how'.** Loads of motivational books and law of attraction trainings say that 'the how is not your business', as in you shouldn't worry about that but instead focus on what you want, and take inspired actions to

get there. But at the same time, I love a good inspiring 'how can I do that?' list. I try for fifty points. I write down my goal, or maybe it's a short-term chunk of a bigger goal, and ask myself *How*. When you do this in a sparky, silly, light-hearted state of mind, you will come up with fun ideas, outrageous ones, and useful prompts too. Write them all down – don't filter or judge – and once you get to fifty, sit back with satisfaction. One or two will jump out at you *and that's really all it takes*. What I find with motivation is that it's always helpful to keep topping up, and creating a 'how' list is just another fabulous tool for your success.

23. **Finish off *all* your loose ends**. When there is unfinished admin, laundry piled up, items to return and jobs to be done, I feel *so drained*. There is no creative energy for anything. And at the same time, I can't be bothered doing any of those jobs. It's a bad cycle! To extricate myself from this low-vibe spiral down to nowhere good, I start working through all those annoying tasks. The crazy thing is, once I get into them I start to feel really good. And then when I finish a few tasks I feel even better. I clean up untidy areas and hotspots, get all my banking up to date, file any paperwork, tidy my fridge, make phone calls and appointments that I've been putting off for no reason. And then, wow! My enthusiasm for everything

reappears. I feel good again! If you need to, make a big list of everything that is annoying you and start ticking them off. Lists can become just another thing that hangs over me, so I sometimes do things without writing them down. It doesn't matter how you approach it, if you are feeling flattened, drained, and bothered, tidy up your loose ends. You only need to start with one, then another, and another!

24. **Totally immerse yourself in your goal**. Just like language immersion works when you move to a new country, so too consider goal immersion. When you have decided on a goal that you know will improve the quality of your life, whether it's becoming slimmer and fitter, saving for a house or paying yours off, immerse yourself in that goal. Read books on the topic every day, give yourself pep talks in the shower or your journal, watch television programs or YouTube videos on the subject, and dream of your vision when you've reached that goal. Visualize how good your life is going to be! Keep this immersion going indefinitely. Remember what you want. Keep your goal right in front of you every day. This is how you will get there!

25. **Kick out your BS excuses**. What invalid and illogical excuses do you carry around with you that you believe will definitely preclude you from achieving a particular goal or living your dream life in general? They will immediately come to mind for you when you ask yourself why you can't have this thing, so write them all down. And then, set about disproving them like you are being paid to. You are the research scientist saying, 'Well, actually, other people are in this same position and they have done it.' Go through each 'obstacle' one by one and show how they are actually *lies*. To help bolster your counterclaims, search out others who have done what you want to do. Borrow their faith and use it to show your BS excuses the door. You are no longer willing to believe them and you don't have to.

26. **Don't be a dog on a thistle**. My dad used to say this to me when I complained about something but did nothing to fix it. Can you picture this dog sitting on a thistle yowling because it's prickly, when he could just stand up and be okay again? My dad's message was don't mope around complaining about your lot. If you want something to be different, change it. Decide what you are no longer available for and do something else. What you chose in the past has led you to where you are

right now and if you want something else in the future, you have to choose differently now. It's a simple enough concept, but oh how we make it so difficult at times! But now you know. You can get up off that thistle and fix something that is bothering you. Do it! Listen to Neil (that's my dad, may he rest in peace)!

27. **'I was born lucky'**. Keep this as your mantra and repeat it to yourself. Write it down somewhere where you will see it often. Say it so often that you begin to believe it and not just think it's a slogan on a coffee cup. You were born lucky! How amazing is that? And then take it as far as you want to go. There is no glass ceiling when you are born lucky. There is no limit on how wonderful your life can be. When you repeat 'I was born lucky' to yourself or see it written somewhere, you will immediately feel empowered, emboldened, and uplifted. It is your own personal source of mental helium. *Choose to believe that you were born lucky* – repeat it, absorb it, infuse it into your very being – and watch your life shift very, very quickly.

28. **The secret to getting ahead is getting started**. Have you heard this phrase before? It's such a good one, and *so true*. Want to start saving for a house deposit? Open a bank account and set up an automatic payment into

it each payday. Want to become slimmer and healthier? Reinvent your grocery trip and only bring home food (and drink) that the healthful, slender you would consume. There is no magic secret to anyone who achieves anything in their life – it's a simple matter of deciding and following through. So, what do you really want right now? Choose, and get started. Let's go!

29. **Be open to the next evolution of your dream life**. What you want now may not be what you want in the future and that's exactly how it should be. You don't want to stay in one place all your life do you? Running on the spot? Wouldn't you rather be open to tasting all flavours of life? When my husband and I lived in the big city, one day a vision came into my mind of us living in the small country town where I grew up. Eventually this change happened, and now that we are here living on a 4-acre property and have been for the past several years, I can feel the next vision coming on. Of downsizing to a smaller property, maybe even an apartment. I can even see the décor. It's going to be very minimal and modern, far different from where we live now. And travelling more once our pets are gone and my husband has retired from his job. It's wonderful to always have something to look forward to at the same time as enjoying where

you are right now.

30. **Raise your vibration**. Inspire yourself every day by doing things that feel good – journaling, reading a favourite book, making notes from an idea that comes to you, imagining your wonderful future and how amazing it's going to be, appreciating how far you have come already, browsing a gorgeous magazine or glossy picture book, people-watching. The more you do these seemingly frivolous things, the more you will realise just how important they are for your spirit. And, the more ideas you come across or dream up, the more will be sent to you. Feeling good and finding inspiration comes from everywhere; all you have to do is *soak it in*. Luckily this feels amazing, like a warm bath for your mindset!

31. **'I get to have it all'**. Imagine if you took this as your life's motto. It's not that it is a greedy thing, but that you get to have everything in your life exactly how you'd prefer it to be. Your health is on point. Your wardrobe reflects how you'd like to see yourself. You have money available for what is important to you. Your relationships are harmonious. You have very little stress or anxiety in your daily life. You have ironed out any irritations that may have bothered you in the past. Taking on the belief that you get to have it all will serve you in so

many ways and open up portals that you never knew existed. It might not feel like a comfortable fit right now, but just try it on and see if you can get used to it!

32. **Practice your dream lifestyle as often as you can**. The things that you imagine you'll do 'One day when', do them now. The clothes you wear, words you say to yourself and others, the way you eat, how you carry yourself, the schedule you keep, practice all these things now as much as possible. By doing them you are bringing the future to you here right now, today. It seems basic, but it is the little things you do every day that can have the greatest impact on your journey and how good you feel about yourself. For me, this looks like eating healthier by making myself salads and fresh fruit bowls, reading, and going for a walk in the sun 'just because'.

33. **You can do it**. Believe that having the life of your dreams is entirely possible for you. Keep this thought in mind and affirm regularly to yourself that it is achievable. Don't listen to others who have negative thoughts ('Come on, be realistic'). You don't have to correct them or try to change their mind, just close your ears to their point of view (because that's all it is – their point of view, *not* fact) and change the subject to something else. Don't even give

them ammunition in the first place. Dream up your beautiful life and start putting plans into action without feeling the need to broadcast what you're doing. Plant your secret garden with lots of fun plans, dreams and wishes and make it so fabulous in there that you don't need anybody else's validation for how you desire to live.

34. **Keep on going**. I took this as a motto for myself for whatever goal I was focusing on. At the time, the goal was weight loss and a healthier lifestyle. That way, when things felt tough, or I forgot I even wanted to be my healthiest self in the first place, I didn't give up. I kept on going. When you hit a few bumps in the road, it's not the time to quit, it's time to *recommit to your vision*. And by reminding yourself to 'keep on going', it is reiterating a message that if you do, *you will get there*. When you keep on going you will eventually reach your goal, no matter how long it takes. The time will pass anyway, so why not make yourself proud?

35. **Find your focus**. What is the one thing that would make the biggest difference in your life? Is it finding a partner, losing weight, or getting your finances sorted? Find your one thing and focus on it as a priority. When you do this, it is much easier to move ahead quickly. Listen to

podcasts, watch YouTube videos and read books on the topic. Make your journalling all about this one thing that would make the biggest difference to your happiness. And if you don't know what your one thing is, ask yourself, *If I had to guess, what would it be?*

36. **Do what you say you are going to do.** Henry Ford said, 'You can't build up a reputation on what you are going to do' which is such a good saying. Would you rather be known as someone who is always talking a big game but never makes a move (we probably know people like that, or eek, maybe that's how we see ourselves?) or as someone who gets things done? I know who I'd choose to be but sometimes it's not as easy as that – we all have our off days. But if we can follow through on what we say we want more often than not, it will become a habit that gathers momentum over time. We will let ourselves down less often, and in turn our self-esteem will rise. Enhance your reputation with yourself and others by identifying as someone who gets things done.

37. **Be more productive than anyone else you know.** There is no magic trick to this, and you don't have to tire yourself out by working relentlessly, but there is a magnetic effect that comes into play when you decide to be a more

productive person. Some days I'll get nothing much achieved yet I've felt very 'busy'. And others, those unicorn days, I've done everything I wanted to – and more – and felt calm and happy all day. I realised that when I felt this way it was because I'd chosen to. And by taking on the 'be more productive than anyone else you know' challenge, you will be able to as well. Keep it in mind and you will spend less time mucking around on the computer, and more time effortlessly flitting around tidying up all those annoying loose ends, making traction with projects, and also, amazingly, enjoying yourself along the way. This is how creating your dream life can be *fun*. It's fabulous!

38. **'You will never receive criticism from someone doing better than you.'** Keep this in mind as you work towards your goals, and especially when you receive critical remarks or well-meaning 'feedback'. When I have received unsolicited advice about what type of books I 'should' write or how a woman my age 'should lift weights' (seriously!) I thank them, and do what I would have done anyway, but I also think, 'Have you written any books?' or 'Are you in amazing shape?' With anyone who offers up their (sometimes belittling thoughts), it is often the case that you would not wish to trade places with them in that area,

so there is no need to heed their 'advice'!

39. **Be 'lightly structured'.** Whether it is a specific goal you wish to achieve such as weight loss, or a general becoming more successful in all areas of your life, you would do well to hold everything you do in a loose grip. Don't make something a strict regime, no fun, or yourself miserable in the pursuit of happiness. It makes no sense! Instead, hold a vision that excites you *so much* in front of you at all times. Step towards it daily, but loosely. If you are someone like me who thinks 'I'll be strict for two months' and then the exciting plan is discarded because the novelty has worn off, this 'new' way of being will seem like a revelation. It certainly was for me!

40. **Live a life of purpose and positivity.** Bounce out of bed every day with these two words in mind. Increase your energy and output with ease by always looking at the bright side of life, and of following what lights you up. There is no way you can't do well when you approach things from this angle. No matter the task at hand, you will do it quicker and more enjoyably too. For me, this phrase is highly motivating and helps me effortlessly get my tasks done as well as my book writing. Take it on for yourself and see how your success in daily living increases immeasurably!

41. **Be inspired by other's successes**. A guy on a house flipping programme I was watching said, 'I think it's really important to get out there and see what the competition's doing. Always look for great ideas and put them together to make them your own.' I took this message on in my own life to look for fresh ways of approaching things which might spark off a new idea for myself. It's great to read of people doing well and how they did it, whether it is in their general views on life or how they achieved a specific goal. You can also gain inspiration from reading autobiographies, and watching or listening to interviews of people who have achieved what you are aiming for, or in areas of your own personal interests.

42. **'Change what you get a kick out of'**. This is such a great mindset shift to help you more effortlessly achieve your desired goals. Say you love eating. You can't imagine anything more enjoyable and don't want to deprive yourself even though you really want to lose weight. So let's think about what is enjoyable about being slimmer: feeling good about yourself, dressing well and looking better, being healthier both now and when you are older, having it be more comfortable to move, and less aches and pains. There are tons of things! Choose one that appeals most to you, and focus on that. Get a kick out of dressing like a slim fashionista, or

of being a picture of health. Or maybe you love buying things but want to pay off your credit card once and for all. Choose to get a kick out of saving money instead: be inspired by people who have paid off their debts and are now saving for a house. Whatever the greatest desire for you is right now, swap it around and get a kick out of the opposite. Focus on *that*!

43. **Become the CEO of your life**. Imagine if your life was an organisation – mine would be The Fiona Company. And within, you would have many different departments: the health department, the finance department, the home department, the love department, the career or job department. How fun does that sound! And you're in charge of everything! As the CEO, you would want to oversee all these various components of your company and ensure they are running smoothly. Because if any of the departments are not going well it's not good for business. Just simple things like looking at the finance department and making sure it's not spending more money than is coming in. Or the health department that enough fresh fruit and vegetables are being delivered to that floor, and are being used up! It's a little bit silly, but I often find that looking at things from a different angle can give us insights or *Ahas* that can help us a lot.

44. **Look for ways to be delighted**. Something that has helped me increase my happiness, success, good luck, and abundance in my life is to always be looking for the good. It doesn't come naturally to me and I still have to remind myself sometimes, but the more I do it the easier it gets. When you choose to be that glass-half-full person, you will find opportunities open up around you that will astound you, you will have money land in your lap, and your relationships will improve as well. Yes, you still have to deal with annoying, boring, realistic things in life too, but even they become less irritating and just something that needs to be handled in a matter-of-fact way. Then you can move onto the next thing and continue to be your delighted, happy self.

45. **Listen to music in preference to the news**. Many people I know like to have the radio or television on for company. For me, it's just too much noise. The talking interrupts my own thoughts, and it's almost never positive input either. May I suggest keeping soft background music playing as an alternative? I find that instrumental songs soothe me better but you may be different. Even in the car I will either play music or, more often, an audiobook or inspiring audio track. Experiment with this yourself and see how different you feel; I *know* you will feel better – more uplifted, optimistic,

happy, and hopeful.

46. **Be in motion**. Newton's First Law of Productivity says: 'An object at rest will remain at rest, and an object in motion will remain in motion'. Each day *put yourself in motion* and you will then *stay in motion.* It is much easier to get things done when you are already doing things. And equally, when you are having a 'can't be bothered' day, you will find it difficult to get even one task done, however, you can turn this around by *getting into motion.* The law of inertia states that 'starting a task is hard, but once you do, it becomes easier to keep going'. I'm not saying don't rest, because that's different. But be intentional about when you are relaxing, and when you are working. For someone who enjoys what they do but often finds it hard to get going, remembering these laws helps me *a lot*!

47. **Let go of unrealistic life goals** and focus on the ones you can actually achieve. Perhaps there are things in the back of your mind that bring you down. Maybe you always thought you'd learn another language and live in a different country for a while. Or you dreamed of opening a quaint little café. But times have changed, and you might have too. No matter what those old thoughts are, give yourself the chance to start afresh. Perhaps you no longer

desire those dreams but they are still in your mental orbit. Maybe you are now drawn to newer, more current ideas such as living a simple and peaceful life and embracing facets of minimalism. Every day you have permission to choose anew. Discard old ideas and begin from today. Ask what you really want *right now* and go for that.

48. **Enjoy your rewards**. Ralph Lauren said 'A lot of hard work is hidden behind nice things', and it's true. Most people who show outward success have worked hard for it. They've made sacrifices, invested time, energy, and money, and worked long hours in pursuit of their goals. I know for myself that I wrote entire books, and spent months, years even, putting them together with no monetary reward. I had to write the books first and then I *might* get paid for them. And now that I have published twenty-plus books, I do get to stay at home and not go to a job, but it's been several years in the making. Every day though, I am so happy I put in the work. I have created my own self-employed income and it is worth the effort. It's always worth it. Whatever goals you have achieved so far, enjoy their benefits. If you have committed to health, enjoy looking and feeling amazing every day. If you have built up a business, enjoy a few treats with your profits. Life is too short not to. And, if there is still

something you want to do, start the 'hard work' today. You won't regret it!

49. **Begin with the little details**. When you are starting out designing the kind of lifestyle you want, consider that the overall picture is made up of millions of tiny stitches. And you are the craftsperson. This is how you will build the life of your dreams, day by day, habit by habit, and decision by decision. Design it first, then craft it. You might already have a busy life, but there is always room for your dreams. Be protective of your time and streamline where you can. Be efficient when you have tasks to do. Don't fritter away hours on inconsequential pastimes that do not add to your happiness. Sometimes we only do things because we've always done them; I know it's like that for me. Be intentional and bring those small details into your daily picture. Weave components of your 'dream life' into your life right now to create *your* beautiful tapestry.

50. **Be your own coach**. I love following coaches online and learning from them, reading books, and studying courses I have bought too. But there is also immense value in *making yourself your own coach*. Balance out the input with self-reflection, because the person who knows you best is *you*. Journal often and ask insightful questions. Build your own bank

of journal prompts by making them up, searching online for others, and noting down ideas when they flash into your mind. Create your own prompts by asking, 'What have I always wanted to know the answer to?' Coach yourself through situations by seeing things from the other person's angle, forgiving them, moving on and deciding to be the best you can be. When you decide that *you* are the best coach you'll ever have, you will be. You are enough in yourself. You have it all right there inside you. Simply ask for the answers and they will come to you, sooner or later. Be patient too! You have a lifetime to perfect yourself!

51. **Create your ideal daily routine**. Do you work better in the morning? Or is nighttime when you come alive? If you don't ask yourself these important questions and simply follow along with someone else's blueprint, you might be making yourself miserable. If someone asked me to write from 9pm to midnight, I'd think they were crazy. I start getting sleepy around 8.30pm and am happily tucked up in bed by 9.15pm. But if you asked me to set my alarm for 5am or 6am to write for three hours, I'd be there with a big smile on my face. For a night owl, this would be torture! I have worked out that for me, I have to do all the things I want to do as early in the day as

possible. And it's easier for me then too. So I do this, and any appointments or outings I book in for after lunch. When you figure out when you work best, easiest, and happiest, life becomes a whole lot better.

52. **Write down your top ten goals every day**. Motivational author and speaker Brian Tracy taught me this. He says to write them out every day without referring back to them so that over time, your true goals will come out. I have many small notebooks filled with my top ten goals, and occasionally I will come across them and flick through a few pages. It's actually quite incredible how many are now part of my daily life. Where we live, what I do for a living, how our home is decorated, and the relationships in my life. This is something you can do today: find a notebook and date the page, then list your top ten goals that you'd love to achieve. They can be short-term or long-term, big or small, it doesn't matter. Brian says there is magic between pen and paper. Writing down your goals cements them in your mind. You have nothing to lose so why not try?

53. **Journal lists of ideal ways you'd love to be**. A fun journalling prompt is to take all the various categories in your life, and then fill them in with wonderfully inspiring ideas for

your idealistic future self. I have a ring binder with many pages – some decades old, and it's enjoyable to read through as well as add a new page to. Categories might include looks, home, dining, personal style, grooming, finances, work, travel, creative life and inspiration, entertaining, fun and recreation, health and nutrition, important people in your life, self-development, self-esteem, and demeanour. Coming up with your own bespoke categories can be part of this exercise too. As you build your pages, you will see your dream life blossom before your eyes.

54. **'This is who I am now'**. Recently I watched the second series of a show called 'The Bear', which is set in a restaurant. One of the characters, Richie, was so annoying that I almost wished he wasn't in the show. He was like the disruptive, naughty kid in class. The restaurant owner sent him away to spend a week working at a Michelin-starred restaurant and he hated being the lackey there, doing jobs such as polishing the forks. But by the end of the week, simply by being around staff who were passionate to provide an exquisite service for their customers, he was a changed man. He arrived back at his old job wearing a suit and tie. He held himself differently. He had raised his standards of how he spoke, worked, and yes, dressed. When colleagues quizzed him he

said, 'I wear a suit now'. And if asked further, he said, 'I just feel better about myself when I do'. Can I tell you, Richie went from being my least favourite character to one of my favourites. And it gave me a shot in the arm too; it made me think, I can do this as well. We all can. We can change if we want to. We get to set our own rules. We get to decide who we're going to be today. And we don't need to justify it to anyone.

55. **Approach life with confidence**. Have you ever noticed that on any reality competition shows such as American Idol, it's always the performers who go out there like they're already famous who do the best job? They believe in themselves so much that the judges and audience buy into it too. And so it is with us. Any goals we have, an event we are nervous about going to, or a project we want to complete, we would have a far better chance of success if we acted like we'd already 'made it'. If we gave ourselves just five minutes of 'pumping up' daily, we would believe in ourselves and have a much better chance of getting to where we want to go. Next time you are anxious about a job interview or contemplating an enticing goal, come at it from an angle of complete confidence and 'act as if'. You're not trying to fool anyone, you're simply giving yourself the best chance of

success within an environment of confidence.

56. **Always be consistently moving** towards your goals. I have found that the areas I am successful in are also the ones in which I have taken consistent daily actions. Healthy living by shopping for good foods and prepping them for easy meals, doing a little exercise every day, and ensuring I get enough sleep. And with my books, I write most days too. People say to me that they could never write a book, but it's not this mythical thing. If you sit down and write each day, eventually you will have a book! It just seems daunting if you look at it as a whole. When you identify your greatest goals and do something towards them every day, you will get there. Being consistent may well be one of the greatest success 'secrets' around!

57. **Lessen your thoughts by moving your body**. For those of us who are prone to procrastination, anxious thinking, and a feeling of stuckness, it may be that we are spending too much time in our head. Our body is still and our mind is busy, which is actually the opposite of what is healthy for us. When there is less on our mind, life feels lighter. But how can we achieve this? *By moving our physical body more.* Not just with exercise, but also in general. If I've spent a long time sitting at the computer, it feels better to get up

and do tasks that require moving around. I find that doing this releases the stuck energy. It really is as if a car has been sitting there with its wheels spinning when you sit for too long! Even just standing up for a tall stretch with your hands over your head feels wonderful. Dr Henry C. Link said it well: 'We generate fears while we sit; we overcome them with action.' I take from this both moving around, and also taking action on something that is weighing on me.

58. **Stoke enthusiasm for your goal**. Maybe you aren't that excited about your goal, well you are, but it's more of an apprehension that you won't achieve it. Especially if it's something you've tried before, such as weight loss or stopping shopping. Try changing your views on looking after your health or your money: think of it as fun and exciting, and that doing this will be the gateway to a fabulous life. Think of being slimmer and healthier, or with a full bank account and an empty credit card as the thing you are after and focus on that. Remind yourself daily. Visualise all the fun things you'll be able to do; how free it will feel. This is how working towards your goals can be fun and exciting, not a boring drag. Rekindle your fire regularly and keep your enthusiasm burning. Let inspiration fuel you!

59. **Look at all you have to gain**. It's easy to have fun ideas of achieving all our goals and living our dream life, but sometimes it's… hard. And we feel lazy. We don't want to put in the effort. We feel like we're going to have to sacrifice too much so we don't even try. I definitely have days like that. In fact I had one yesterday! Thank goodness I am back to my usual happy self today. But part of how I got out of that little hole I'd temporarily fallen into, was to instead of thinking of deprivation and how hard it was going to be, was to look at all I would be *gaining*. I fell asleep last night going through a big list in my head of all the goodness that is to come. And it worked! It's occurred to me before that success is simply a matter of keeping on going towards your goal, using whatever mental tricks necessary. And if that's what it takes, I'm all for it, because it's worth it. And to see that, just look at *all you have to gain.*

60. **Always be learning**. When I'm driving in the car, it's not the radio that is playing, I'll be listening to an audiobook or some other non-fiction audio content on topics that interest me. Occasionally I will listen to a fiction audiobook but mostly I'm learning something new. I remember Brian Tracy talking once about 'making your drive time learning time' and that if you multiply your average commute

by the number of days in a year you will find a huge amount of time in which to enrich your brain. And it's effortless too; you don't have to be sitting there studying a book, it is sinking in effortlessly while you drive to or from work. Or the supermarket. Or school drop-off. It's an easy way you can plug extra inspiration in, and the content can be tailored to your desired lifestyle – you might listen to a health TED Talk one day, a personal finance audiobook after that, and a fashion masterclass next, etc. For those of us who got a little bored with school and its mostly dry topics (in my schooling days of the 1980s anyway), it is a revelation when we hop back into learning in the Internet era. Even just YouTube alone has an incredible wealth of knowledge, for free! And if you pay for Premium (I do and love it), you won't get ads and you can download videos to play offline so you don't chew up your data listening in your car while you're out.

61. **Move quickly on a great idea** when you have a brain flash – speed is essential in your new successful life. I have heard people say that if you don't do something straight away, you will never do it, and I have found this to be true for me as well. Even right down to the simple things such as buying a product to use. If you don't try it the very next time you have the chance to or even as soon as you get home,

it will probably sit in your cupboard for ages and then you'll declutter it. You can't deny it! And for 'move forward' ideas such as 'I might try paleo', 'I'm going to start my book dream by putting together a brief outline of what it might be about', 'I'm going to clean out my closet today so that I'm excited about fashion again', or 'I'm going to try slow and steady and lose five pounds by Christmas instead of my usual strict, short-lived regime'. Whatever inspired idea you receive in your mind, put it into action immediately. Whether it is something big or small, I assure you that you will be thrilled with the results.

62. **Seek only positive in the world**. Cultivate a deep sense of inner peace by looking at all the goodness around you. Every day endeavour to make your life calm and soft by soaking in your good luck at being born you. Being this way will help with appreciation and gratitude, and you will find yourself more effortlessly attracting good things into your life. Life is too short to feel tense daily, or always be waiting for the cartoon anvil to drop on you. It won't. Yes of course life is full of situations to deal with but don't pre-empt them. Stay focused, stay positive, and enjoy the ride. I have been doing this and it feels so much better than waking up with a 'here we go again, what does today have for me?' attitude, even if there have

been a few bumps in the road lately. There will *always* be bumps in the road, but when you keep yourself light, soft and airy, you will feel them less. Just like shock absorbers or suspension in a car! Infuse your soul with positivity and *allow it to cushion your journey.*

63. **Seek inspiration from unexpected places**. Two people who consistently inspire me with their go-ahead attitude are Kris Jenner and Kim Kardashian. When I'm in the mood I enjoy an episode of The Kardashians for a little Los Angeles glam lifestyle, but what I always come away with is their motivation to live how they want to live. And I get to do that too – really design what my dream lifestyle looks like and be happy to work hard to get it. For me this means keeping my life simple, staying on top of my admin and household tasks, and putting in the time writing my books, not just 'think' about writing my books. (You know what I mean, I'm sure!) There are interviews with Kris and Kim on YouTube and it's impressive how focused and driven they are. I don't desire their exact lifestyle or over-the-top looks, but I can enjoy them nudging me along to be more glamorous and successful, and also not to worry so much what others may think about how I live my life. Thanks girls!

64. **Be sweet and kind always**. While you are going for your goals and building your dream life, there is no need to be anything other than the lovely person you already are. You don't need to turn into someone different as you reach your next level of success, even if you are really going for it! I know I can worry about losing my softness, or of becoming ruthless. While still on the subject of Kim Kardashian, I have read in many articles about her and of fan meetings too, that she is the sweetest, kindest person in real life. I don't think I've ever read of an encounter where she is rude or dismissive. Considering how famous she is, that's quite impressive. And also a relief for some of us, who may be subconsciously keeping ourselves at the same level because we don't want to get too big-headed or 'too big for our boots'. Any of the bigs! So keep your calm and lovely demeanour and know that you don't have to sacrifice it as you get ahead in life. Phew!

65. **Work hard now** so you can set yourself up for the rest of your life. No matter if you are married, in a relationship or single, it's ultimately *your* job to take care of your future. When you think from this angle, it's easier to stop mindless spending. Instead, you're pondering if you should set up an investment account and deposit $50 into it by automatic

payment each month, or how you can start a side hustle. Come up with ways you can both *cut costs* (of things that aren't necessarily adding to your life), and *make more money* by opening an Etsy store, starting a YouTube channel, or finally writing 'your book'. From someone who never thought they could be self-employed, I'm telling you it's not that hard. Just try something. Go for something you've never had the guts to do before. Publishing my first book was mildly terrifying, but now with twenty plus books on Amazon, it's a fun and exciting game, and I get to live my dream simple life writing from my home office with just my pets for company while my husband is at work. Whatever kernel of a dream is inside you, nurture it and give it a go. If you never try, you'll never know.

66. **Find someone who is doing exactly what you want to do**, and 'employ' them as your mentor. Maybe they have a book or an online course so you really can learn directly from them, but even if they don't, you can still follow their social media profiles, search for written articles, or listen to interviews with them. And if they are someone in your real life rather than an online personality, chat with them, offer to help, or invite them out for coffee. Most people are thrilled to pass along their advice to others. To inspire myself as an author, I will buy

Kindle books, watch YouTube videos, and tear out magazine articles of famous authors. I love to read their tips and how they structure their day. No matter what form my 'research' takes, there is always a new takeaway, or an idea to be sparked off from something they have said.

67. **Own how beautiful you are inside and out**. Being a chic success is not just about making money and growing a business. Having confidence and good self-esteem, being self-assured, and being happy in your own skin will give you such a glow and really project your best self out to people in your orbit. Others will be drawn to you from not only your radiant looks, but the goodness in your heart as well. Aim to be beautiful from both the inside *and* the outside. Carry yourself with confidence, practice being non-judgemental of yourself and others, and have a good sense of humour. To assist, give yourself high-quality fuel, exercise often for your rich lady glow, and prioritise beauty sleep. Can you imagine how a lady who shows up like this would be received by others? And how serene and happy she would be in herself? It's worth aiming for, right?

68. **Believe in magic**. To create what you want in your life, choose to believe in magical things happening. I love to be practical, organised, work hard, and write down my goals, but I also love the feeling of fairy dust sprinkled all around me. I swear, I can almost hear the tinkling bell noise sometimes! It comes from cultivating a positive attitude, looking for the goodness in everything, and expecting things to turn out for the best. At times when I've gotten stuck in a problematic situation, I remember that I believe in magic. I pull myself out of the wallowing, and ask for the issue to be resolved. Within a day or two, maybe a week at the most, as long as I keep staying on the positive side, my prayers are answered. It's quite incredible. There is room for both the hustle *and* the ethereal. Those who don't believe in magic will never find it, so figure out a way for *you* to believe in the fairy dust, however you need to work it or picture it.

69. **Make your life wonderful**. None of us are perfect, and we all have niggles in our life, I know I do. Mine are small right now, but in the past they have been big. But what I do know is that in order to be happy and successful, if there is something I don't like that's going on in my life, I figure out how to fix it. No-one wants to listen to me sitting and complaining about it forever – least of all me! So I take all

the things that are bothering me, or maybe focus on one if it's a bit bigger, and make it into a goal. I brainstorm all the ways I can improve upon or eliminate this issue for good. I keep my desired outcome as a focus. I'll do things in support of it daily. Work towards your overall desire to live a wonderful life and iron out all the little kinks as much as possible. The more you iron, the less there will be!

70. **Commit to your dream life.** You have to stay committed. Most people start out, often on January 1st, with a big list of New Year's resolutions. Apparently the 17th of January is the date pretty much everyone has given up or forgotten about their dreams. If you don't want to be like 'most people' commit to what you started. Re-read your goals. Do what it takes to live your dream life. Remember how awesome it is going to be! Re-write your vision if it gets a little stale. Start over often. Look at today's date and consider that to be the day you begin. Consider your home, your car and how you dress to be your 5D vision board. Bring elements of your dream life into your current reality. Stay the course, it's worth it!

71. **Keep your plans private**. It's fun to talk about your goals, dreams, and desires, but I've found that it's *more* fun to show people your results instead. And to do so in a nonchalant

fashion. It's so enjoyable! So, rather than tell everyone how you're on a diet and going to be your goal weight by the end of the year, move in silence and just go about your life. Then, at the family Christmas dinner where you haven't seen your cousins since last year, they can exclaim about how good you look. Be reserved and private. Have mystique. Let your plans fuel you rather than letting the air go when you talk about them. I know it can be a hard thing to do for those of us who are naturally sharers! But just try it, maybe with one goal. You will be amazed at how you streak ahead. It's almost like the contained energy is propelling you along.

72. **Empower yourself with your goals**. Something fun that happens when you map out your dream life and start working towards it, is that you feel empowered, hopeful, and *strong*. It really does feel like you are steering your own ship! And this feeling of empowerment leads to even greater things. It's a beautiful momentum. The opposite is feeling like nothing will make a difference in your life so why even try. Urgh, I so know that feeling from flat days. That's why I am all about boosting myself up with happy, positive thoughts and feelings, of doing things that feel good, and going for my goals. And they might be tiny goals too, like keeping up to date with

the laundry (this one really makes or breaks my week!)

73. **Follow what makes you sparkle**. In life there will always be an evolution of what you want to do. Inspiration that was exciting before might not even move you now. It's all about finding what really excites you at any given time. When you keep current with your desired flavour of life, and follow the breadcrumbs of what makes you feel happy, you will find that something is sparked off and you are motivated all over again. Our inner happiness is not something that is set once and forgotten about. We are constantly growing and evolving so at least have a say in where you are going! That's why consistent, gentle decluttering is so good. You keep yourself in alignment with where you want to go.

74. **Be someone who does not curse**. I have seen that it's become quite a trend to use curse or swear words, and sometimes it's funny, but often it just makes people – particularly females – just sound coarse, uncouth, and uneducated. Maybe I'm old-fashioned, but I remember the saying about using more intelligent words than a swear word. Of course sometimes one will slip out, but if you never curse usually, this just makes it more endearing. Versus someone who uses curse

words regularly. Choose your language wisely and be a person with an elevated vocabulary. To me, swear words sound cheap, so be someone who is very, very expensive!

75. **Keep bouncing back**. In life, and especially when creating your dream life, you will get knockbacks. Someone might criticise you, or you notice a friend distancing themselves. There will always be setbacks, roadblocks and issues to work around. I mostly receive good reviews from nice people for my books, but occasionally I will get one-or two-star reviews and some can be quite nasty! I always try to learn from my not-so-good reviews, but when someone is horrible it can affect me for days. But it doesn't matter how awful someone is to you, you can choose to just keep bouncing back. Keep returning to yourself and what you desire to achieve. Because what's the alternative? That someone who is having a bad day causes you to give up on what you're going for? If I stopped writing when I received a bad review I wouldn't be here for you today. As long as you are happy with the quality of product you are producing, or sure that the changes you are making are not hurting anyone else, you can quite rightfully keep on going. Be self-possessed, and practice not letting others hurtful comments derail you.

76. **Be specific about what you want**. When you start out with this work, you might not be used to 'asking' for exactly what you want. You might be used to taking whatever life offers you. But if you would get still in your mind and ask yourself *how you really want to live* and write it all down, you will see your life transform in the most magical of ways. Start yourself a big list and write down *all the things*, big and small. You might want a wardrobe worthy of a fashionista, to be in your best shape ever, to go back to school and study for your nursing degree, to reignite the spark in your relationship, to have a perfectly staged pantry, to go out to live theatre more, and to grow a herb garden. Make a gorgeous list of everything you'd love to have in your dream life and then gaze at it in wonder. Wouldn't it be wonderful? And the fab thing is, you *can* have it all. Read through your list often, feel how wonderful it would be to live like this. And choose items from your list to work on. One day in the future, you might chance upon this list and realise you can tick off everything on it. Wouldn't that be something? And it all starts with... dreaming and being specific about what you want.

77. **Find your feeling**. How we desire to feel is a great way to take a 'side door' into creating our dream life. It's an easy, non-threatening way to welcome what we want! For me at the moment, I'd like my life to feel more peaceful and organised. This is so I can write my books as often as I want to without feeling guilty that there are other things I 'should' be doing. Which means I need to focus on decreasing the *clutter* in my life – clutter in my home, cluttery thoughts, and piling too much into my schedule. It will be a season of clearing out in order to feel... peaceful and organised. What about you? How would you like to feel?

78. **Use the Law of Attraction to your advantage**. By identifying desires, your subconscious will start running in the background looking for opportunities and pointing them out to you. Say that you'd love your next vacation to be on a cruise. You've never been on one before and have always wanted to. Before long you will be noticing advertisements for cruises, someone you know will tell you about their upcoming trip, and then one day... you will be standing up on deck looking out to sea. Or if you would love to write a book, you will start noticing all the information online about how to write and publish your book. The key is to stop and notice all the little signposts, and put them to

good use too. This one tip is how you can work on all your goals in an easy and fun way.

79. **Take action**. This is probably the biggest difference between those who achieve success in their life and those who... don't. It all comes down to whether you take action on all those little (or big) ideas you get. You can say affirmations, write down your goals, create your vision boards on Pinterest and dream about how wonderful it is when you get to your goals, but unless you actually get your butt off the chair and do something, you'll get nowhere! I love the saying 'things get done when you do things'. It is certainly motivating and gets me going when I've spent a bit too much time dreaming and not enough time doing. We certainly need the dreaming, but we can't forget the doing. So find one thing today, one thing that pops into your head right now, *and do it*. And take a step towards something you want.

80. **No excuses**. Not every day is the same. For me, some days I need softness, and I will approach my goals this way, which means I'll do my best with the energy I have and the time available. I might have a gentler day. And other days when I have lots of energy, it's 'no excuses' all the way. You might be the same. But no matter your energy levels, holding the

phrase 'no excuses' will help you make better decisions more often than not. Adopt a 'no excuses' policy when it comes to how you live your life. It's just one of the many little mind tricks that can help you raise your standards in every category of your life.

81. **Fit little things in everywhere**. I don't like to have household tasks or admin/personal finance jobs hanging over me. So I have made it my habit to fit those small chores in amongst other things and also to do them as soon as I see them. This helps keep things effortlessly up-to-date and helps me feel on top of my life. It's a great feeling! One example is that I empty the dishwasher in the morning as quick as I can while my NutriBullet smoothie is whizzing (I whizz it for a long time to make it thick and creamy!). I put earplugs in to protect my hearing (it is *loud*) and get unpacking. Or I'll file my grocery receipts or process any bank transfers as soon as they need doing. I'll put a load of laundry on before the baskets are overflowing. Sometimes I'll even do half a load to get ahead of the game. I know all these things are relaxing because I've done them the opposite way before. When there aren't little tasks following you around hanging over your head, energy is freed up to do creative and fun things. You really can feel light as air and as if you are living your dream life.

82. **Create a social media 'burner' account**. You will no doubt have an Instagram or other social media account. What I would propose, is to add a second account which you can use to strengthen your motivation when it comes to your goals. With my second account, which I don't post on, I can feel free to follow whoever is inspiring me at the time, and unfollow them without guilt when my focus changes. So, at one time I might be prioritising getting healthy habits in place so I will follow fitness and health accounts. Then, I might be in a style and fashion phase so will change my feed to reflect that. And sometimes I'll be in a kickass personal success phase and follow all the motivational accounts. When you feel like a scroll, you can go to this account and still be in the zone. It's the best of both worlds!

83. **'Reset' daily**. I love the word 'reset' so much. I'd see people online resetting their 'clean kitchen at night' or doing a 'Sunday reset' to prime themselves for a productive week (meal prepping, getting their outfits organised, doing their laundry, tidying the house etc). But I have found that you can reset anywhere at any time, and it feels so good! And effortless too thank goodness. You can reset your kitchen counter by putting away items that shouldn't be there, and giving the surfaces a wipe down. Reset your bedroom by making the bed and

giving it a quick tidy. Reset your car when you get home by taking everything out, and putting things back too, like your washed keep-cup. Reset your closet by doing laundry and putting it away, ironed and checked for any maintenance required. Reset your office desk by filing receipts, checking your planner is up-to-date, and generally straightening up. When you take on resetting as a way of life, you will always be ready. You won't have chores hanging over you. You will be actively looking around for places to reset!

84. **Be organised as much as you can**. I have come to realise that the more I keep on top of things, the more successful and happy I feel. And conversely, the more I let things slide on a regular basis, the more overwhelmed and bogged down I feel. Hmm, which choice sounds more appealing? And the cool thing is, once you get the momentum going (which happens very quickly once you make the decision), it's easy to keep on going. *An object in motion stays in motion*, as already mentioned in no. 46 is especially apt in this situation. Being organised = the secret to your success. Work out simple ways you can become *next-level organised*. Reduce the inventory in your home (aka decluttering), use what you have, use things up, tidy areas and keep them useable. Make these life-long

regular habits and you will feel like a chic success.

85. **Infuse your life with positive anchors**. In your environment, surround yourself with reminders of your goals and how you want to live. If want to live in an elegant, feminine, and successful way, choose décor items, skincare, clothing, and even little details like your planner or phone cover, to reflect this. You can enhance your home, your workplace (a beautiful coffee cup? Handcream and flowers on your desk?), and even your car. In my car I have a pretty scented Bath & Body Works vent clip, play motivational audio tracks, and change the background lighting to go with the outfit I am wearing (I know, that's next-level nerdy but I love it!) Whatever makes you feel good, do it. There is no detail too small that your subconscious mind can't notice. Have fun with this tip!

86. **Choose to be exceptional**. When I looked up antonyms of mediocre, I came across a wonderful array of words such as excellent, different, extraordinary, first-rate, uncommon, unusual and yes, exceptional. I love the thought of being uncommon, or rare, because being a chic success can be a rare thing these days. Not many people in my life think like me or do the kinds of things I do. But that's

okay, because I choose to be different, and likely so do you if you are reading this book. Don't worry about what others are doing, worry about what *you* are doing. Inspire them with your brilliance and how you live your life exactly as you want to. Follow what lights *you* up and decide that you are going to live an exceptional life, on your own terms of course!

87. **Do life your way**. I love to get up and get going early, because I know I don't have as much oomph left later in the day. I usually rise at 6am with my alarm, but occasionally I will wake earlier. I used to lie there trying to get back to sleep because I didn't want my husband Paul to think I was weird if I got up at that time. Then I just decided, *Why not be true to me and get up early if I want to?* One particular day I'd been up for ages, pottering around with ideas in my office, and decided to paint my nails quickly so they'd dry in time for me to do things later. Paul walked past the door to my office and said 'you are probably the only woman in Hawke's Bay doing her nails at ten to six in the morning' which sounded so funny, but then made me think that was an excellent thing! I encourage you to march to the beat of your own drum too. Don't worry if people think you are strange. It's your life and you get to live it exactly the way it suits you best.

88. **Use your magic wand**. Brian Tracy talks about the magic wand technique, where you journal on your life as if it was perfect, as if you had waved a magic wand and everything suddenly became wonderful – your home life, your finances, your relationships, your body, everything! He suggests you write out in great detail how all these categories would look. I have done this many times over the years and it is so fun to dream, useful, and sometimes surprising. You will find that even though your ideas might change as you repeat the exercise, certain elements remain. Doing this helps refine what you want, and it also implants your desires into your mind so you have a better chance of bringing them to you. I have also found that using my magic wand on problem areas is fabulous too. If I have a handful of bothersome things, I write out a magic wand list in my journal stating them as fixed, completed or resolved. Then I say thank you, and put my journal away, for the mysteries of the Universe to work it's magic.

89. **Create your own success plan**. Let's take one of your goals. Maybe you have had this goal for a long time and it's never really gotten anywhere. But you know that you really want it – so frustrating! We're going to have a little play around, so grab a journal. Firstly, write a page full of all the reasons why you want this

100 Ways to be a Chic Success and Create Your Dream Life

goal. Let's say it's weight loss, so write down what weight you'd love to be and why. Then, write down all the reasons why you think you haven't achieved it yet. And on the third page, write down all the little and big ways you could become your dream weight. This three-step process is such a simple and fun way to create your own success plan, and it will get you going. It will give you a list of fabulous benefits, a look into the shadow side and why you might be self-sabotaging, and also provide a motivating list of ways to be and things to do. Let me know how you get on with it!

90. **Find the answers to your questions.** What questions would you like to know the answers to? If you had a coach sitting right in front of you and she promised she could help you solve any conundrum, what would you ask her? Write all those questions down. Some for me might be: How to have lasting weight loss? How to be able to avoid temptation (food and drink)? How to feel more confident? How to have a wonderfully productive yet relaxing day? And now, my friend, you have the best list of journal prompts ever. Choose one, and start writing everything down that you can think of to answer that question. Creating your own list of journal prompts is such a valuable, fun, and little-known way of inspiring yourself. And, you get to find out answers to the questions

you've always wondered about!

91. **Dress for your dreams**. Don't save your nicer clothes for when you have become slimmer, gotten richer, or landed your dream job. Dress well now. *Dress for the job you want not the job you have* is an excellent piece of advice that I'm sure you already know. For me, I choose to dress as 'a successful author'. I started this years ago by deciding *not* to scribble away in track pants and a messy topknot, even if no-one saw me all day. I activate my inner successful author by wearing my lovely going-out clothes at home, putting a little makeup on each day, doing my hair, and wearing perfume and jewellery too. Doing this changes how you see yourself, and how you feel as well. You feel like a chic success even before anything happens, and that's gotta be a good thing, right? It certainly can't hurt! So dress for your dreams and start the magic happening with your fabulous sparkly energy.

92. **Be happy to be richer**. Does it feel a bit uncomfortable to think about earning more? Do you have a feeling of guilt that if you did this and others can't, you are being greedy? I feel this too. As I have built my work-from-home author lifestyle, I feel bad that I might earn a similar amount to someone who has to go to a job forty hours a week. But we all get to

choose how we live, and maybe by earning more and becoming wealthier you can inspire someone close to you to think differently too. Giving up on your dreams won't help anyone, but doing the important work of feeling uncomfortable sometimes (it means you are growing!) can. Keep doing what you are doing and choose to be a bright shining light (or perhaps a pretty, softly lit candle) so that others can see you to follow you.

93. **Be *your* definition of a chic success**. When I asked myself 'How can I be a chic success?', I got: *Wake up every day happy to be me. Look forward to every day being magical. Enjoy all the goodness that is around me. Be thankful for my good fortune. Work hard and be productive. Have downtime to rest, play, and do self-care. Let others be who they are and not try to control them. Look to myself when I think something should be improved. Be a good steward of my money, time and energy. Do the right thing. Be kind to others and myself. Rejoice in my beautiful selection of clothing as I get dressed in the morning. Make the most of my looks. Be tidy and clean in all areas of my life. Try new things. Do something I've never had the guts to do. Be open-minded and open-hearted.* That's me, but what does *your* inner self say? What is her definition of a chic success and

how can she be it?

94. **Just be you**. If you are looking to build an online business, start an Instagram account, write books, or even just more authentically connect with people in your life, there is no hidden secret that you don't know. *You only need to be you*, and your people will find you. It's so simple and that's why I think people tie themselves up into knots trying to work out what people want from them. I know I did this in the early days of my blog. But if you just be you, the best, happiest and most positive you, your readers, friends, clients and fans will find you. I always put my best foot forward online, I'm not going to 'let it all hang out', but that's only polite to do so. You wouldn't leave your house with unbrushed teeth and hair a mess would you? Of course not. So show up well, but also, show up as *you*. Just be you. Isn't that relaxing to hear? No stress, no effort, just you offering yourself to the world.

95. **Put yourself out there**. There is a small catch to 'just being you', and it's scary to contemplate sometimes. You have to show up and be visible. You have to let people get to know you, the real you. Whether it's on YouTube, in a published article, your social media, or while networking or socialising in real life, it can be nerve-wracking. I have found

it helpful to take small steps at a time – writing a blog post, or sharing a photo online. And you don't have to do anything you don't want to either. I still feel too nervous to do much YouTube, so I don't! Choose something that stretches you, but not too much. Only go as far as you are happy to, but do try something. In real life invite a friend around for coffee, or organise a ladies afternoon tea. Others might feel as shy as you and be thrilled for the invitation!

96. **Choose symbols of your ideal lifestyle.** My ideal lifestyle would be healthy, elegant, and feminine. I have identified a few indulgences I can partake in every day and still be my ideal lady. Not only are they enjoyable, but they remind me of the woman I want to be. Details such as one or two pieces of dark chocolate to close off a meal. Sipping sparkling water before dinner and a small glass of wine *with* dinner. And having decaf coffee with cream, or herbal tea in the evening. When I wanted to slim down, I didn't want to 'just' eat salad and be dull. I wanted to feel richly indulgent as well, so I found a few gems that support this without sabotaging my healthy self goals. Choose words to describe *your* ideal lifestyle and find ways to support them in a positive way.

97. **Give yourself an appealing moniker**. There are loads of fun videos, posts, and articles online and books available too, that have all the latest trendy monikers or nicknames people channel to be their best selves. I've even written a book called '100 Ways to be That Girl' (which continues to be my most popular book). There is the Clean Girl, Rich Girl, being Leveled Up and so on. I love thinking about my Rich Lady Lifestyle (which always comes to mind for me as looking like a 1990s Danielle Steel mini series!) or being a Bestselling Author. Whatever your goals are, give yourself an appealing nickname and *be her*. Make that name your own, and let her help you get ahead faster. Sometimes you can dawdle around, and at other times you want to rocket ahead. Honour both speeds and make it more fun with a bespoke handle. What will yours be?

98. **Who do you want to be?** This is such a good question to ask yourself, and it can take a bit of thinking about, but once you get the hang of it, you will find fabulous information. When I did, I came up with: *A successful stay-at-home wife and author. Stylish and fashionable. Relaxed, calm and happy. In control of myself. Time to relax and read. Food is not my main focus. Living a good life. A simplified home. A clean, lovely home. Enjoying*

homemaking. Reading this gives me a happy, calm feeling, and it helps me come back to what I value and what decisions I make in the future. Who do *you* want to be?

99. **Focus single-mindedly on your greatest goal of the moment**. Just as a magnifying glass can cause grass to be set on fire with the sun's rays, so too can you quantum leap in your progress by putting all you've got into one goal. Make that goal *your everything*. Make it fun. Infuse every aspect of your daily life with it. Read books, watch videos, and study course material on it. Visit the library, search online, and ask people you know how they did it. Whatever resources you have, use them. Keep your goal top of mind by making your screensaver an inspiring image representing this goal. Journal about how amazing it's going to be once you reach your goal. Dress and present yourself as if you already are that person. Use as many different angles as you can, and you *will* get there!

100. **Enjoy the ride**. Abraham Hicks says, 'You can never have a happy ending at the end of an unhappy journey', which is why I like to make everything I do enjoyable, playful, and light. Even if my goal is to lose weight or save money, I look for the fun and easy ways to achieve these things. I simply cannot 'knuckle down'

and endure deprivation and you may be the same. We might be able to work this way for a little while, but before too long we will rebel against our own wishes, and it's simply because we are not making the journey happy. When you figure out how to make the way to your goal a fun place to be, you've found the secret to success. You do get to have the best of all worlds – enjoyment *and* success. Always be asking yourself of any project you wish to work on: How can I make this easier? How can I make this more fun? How can I feel light and playful while I achieve this? It is possible, and your creative mind is waiting for you to ask her. She is ready to go there with you!

Now we have reached one-hundred ways to be a chic success and live your dream life, are you raring to go? Have you already taken a few tips and acted on them? You don't have to memorise every point, or even resonate with all of them.

There might be some that you don't jive with at all, and others that are *love at first sight*. Take those ones and run with them. Wallpaper your bedroom (or at least your phone screen) with them. Write out phrases and words that ring your bell on little pieces of paper and hide them in your wallet.

Be that girl who has her head in the clouds and her feet on the ground. Dance in your mind and see all the pretty balloons that are floating around above you. Let yourself catch one of the ribbons holding them and lift up into the sky like Peter Pan. Dream of the macaron tower that is your magical life and build it one macaron at a time.

Don't listen to the naysayers who say you are only deluding yourself because you are a positive thinker. Wouldn't you rather be delusional than... *normal*?

There is too much normalness around for my liking. It colours everything grey and holds us back. Life needs dreamers like you and me. And even if the only person we are affecting is us, that is the most important person!

We can only control ourselves. We don't need to exhaust ourselves organising everyone else. Unless they are children or pets of course, we need to look after them. But for everyone else, everyone who is over the age of eighteen, they get to live their life. They may be *in* our life, but we don't need to try and manage them. It's enough to manage ourselves don't you think?

So float up, feel free and unencumbered, and build the life of your dreams. You only get one life, so why not make it a display of fireworks, champagne, sparklers and bouquets of lush peonies. How's that for a visual?

I'll see you on the beach, or in the café, or the hotel lobby bar. We'll be the ones virtual-toasting to our chic success, in whichever flavour we have chosen!

50 Success Habits of the Chic, Go-Ahead Woman

Yes! Because, why not?

One of the absolute best questions to ask when you are designing your dream life is:

'How would 'she' be?'

As in:
How would that chic and successful woman spend her days?
*How would she live **her** dream life?*
*What **is** her dream life?*
What habits does she have?
What kinds of foods does she eat?
Who are the people she surrounds herself with?
What are her thoughts like?

How does she dress?
What does she value most?
What kind of demeanour does she have?
What are her behaviours?
What does she do in the morning? The evening?
How does she ideally spend her weekends?

It is *so* fun and empowering to go through every single part of 'her' life and imagine how she is in each area. With 'she' being the lady who is living your dream life a.k.a. the future you. You get to focus on the version of yourself that you want to become *and design her from the ground up.*

Then, and this is the genius part, you start doing what *she* does. You bring elements of your future dream life into your real daily life. Not only will those ways of being be how you are in the future, but by doing them today is how you will get there.

So to finish this book and give you an extra boost towards creating your dream life, please enjoy fifty chic habits a successful woman would infuse into her life.

This is how she does it! Yeah!

1. **She cultivates self-control** in all areas of her life, especially those categories in which she has traditionally struggled in. She sees restraint and discipline as the key to her freedom, not her captor. She loves identifying as someone with

self-control and of being a self-possessed woman.

2. **She takes time to dream every day**. She journals about her future. She practices being in it. She falls asleep at night visualising all the goodness that is to come, at the same time as being deeply grateful for her life as it is today.

3. **She dresses as her future self would**. If her future self is slimmer or richer, she dresses that way now. She enjoys wearing the kinds of clothes she imagines herself in 'one day when'. If she sees herself wearing floaty summer dresses when she is slimmer, she finds a flattering dress for now. If she imagines shopping at high-end stores when she is richer, she chooses similar styles and colours from stores in her current budget range.

4. **She takes exquisite care of her physical body**. She enjoys luxurious baths or showers with beautifully scented products. She keeps her bathroom products clean and curated. She wears fragrance that makes her feel like she is 'there'. She washes and blow-dries her hair so it shines, and takes that extra ten minutes to do so. She shapes and polishes her nails once a week, whether she prefers classic red, sheer nude, or neatly buffed.

5. **She has a vision for her environment and leans towards that**. In her dreams she has an idealistic view of her home to be elegant and luxurious, and she as the lady of the house. No matter her budget she keeps this in mind as she cleans and tidies her abode, and adds little touches to remind her of her vision.

6. **She relates to others in a way that makes her feel good**. She offers help when genuinely needed, otherwise she stays in her lane and lets others live *their* lives too. She is kind and caring, but she does not smother people. She lets them be them.

7. **She is enthusiastic about her goals**. She dreams them up, journals on them, makes fun steps to carry them out, and takes inspired action towards them. When she gets an idea, she does something about it right then. She is *in love* with the creation of her dream lifestyle, and it shows in her results. But most importantly, she enjoys herself every step of the way.

8. **She looks after herself**. Even if in a happy relationship she looks out for her own best interests, by knowing where her money is at, and keeping herself 'safe'. She has seen other women left in dire financial circumstances and she does everything she can to never be in that position.

9. **She enjoys being 'different' to others**. Her biggest fun in life is zigging when others are zagging. She marches to the beat of her own drum and follows her own path. She has taken on 'To thine own self be true' as her personal motto. It doesn't matter to her if something is fashionable or not, if she loves it, she loves it.

10. **She knows if others can do it then so can she**, and all it takes is for her to decide what she wants, and follow through. When she found out it really was that simple it was if every door in the Universe suddenly opened up to her.

11. **She loves being self-driven**. While others are playing, she is plotting. She dreams up fun plans for the future, whether it's the next evolution of her wardrobe style, retirement travel, updating her home, or a creative hobby project.

12. **She chooses not to compare herself with others**, because she knows she has many strengths, skills, and talents, and they will be different to other peoples. She keeps her blinkers on and focuses on what *she* can offer the world.

13. **She identifies as a superstar**. She knows she is meant for great things, both big and small. She feels the sparkle inside, and lives to spread

her love.

14. **She borrows from her library of inspiration**. Books and audiobooks, favourite movies and television series, journal prompts, motivational quotes, Pinterest boards… whatever she is in the mood for, she knows she can call on support from any number of different sources in an instant.

15. **She pays herself first**. So she can give from her overflow of energy, money and time, she keeps her cup full. Good food, nourishing rest, play time, happy relationships, and an environment of peace, calm and order all do this for her.

16. **She is positive and happy as much as possible**. When she looks at the bright side of things it is easier to feel abundant and like she is living her dream life already.

17. **She doesn't pay too much attention to the down days**. She knows they will always pop up from time to time, but also she knows that, like clouds, they will pass. Those days are not the time to focus on difficulties, but to visualise, think, and dream of everything that is good. And lose herself in a favourite movie!

18. **She sets little themes for her days**. On a cozy day she might enjoy nesting and making things pretty around the house, and relaxing with a book. And on productive days she sets herself alight with her output. On any given day she asks herself, 'What is my theme for today?'

19. **She identifies habits** which are moving her *away* from her dream life, and tries to replace them with habits which move her *towards* her dream life. It takes a little effort, but often it's a simple switch that helps do this.

20. **She consumes material that makes her feel happy**. Books, movies, television series, YouTube videos; they all have a common thread. They are uplifting, motivating, enjoyable, humorous, or inspiring. Depressing or frightening media has no place in her world.

21. **She stays in her lane**. She knows it is no business of hers what other people think of her. Whenever she gets too involved in others lives she gently reminds herself that they get to do them, and she should focus on herself. And when others try to veer into her lane she simply thanks them and carries on doing what she was already doing.

22. **She stays ready**. She keeps her looks on point, her clothes laundered and hanging in her closet,

and her home 'company-ready'. This is something she has practiced and built up over the years so now it is second-nature to her. She never needs to scramble because she *stays ready*.

23. **She is willing to put in the effort** for anything she wants to achieve, because she knows that the harder she works, the 'luckier' she gets!

24. **She cultivates her own motivation**. No matter what she is doing that day, she knows she needs to get her mindset on board. She pumps herself up with positive words, reads a few pages of a favourite uplifting book, and visits her inspiring Pinterest boards. All these little reminders add a glittering quality to her day, and help her feel like she is living her dream life.

25. **She creates the feeling of 'vacation every day'**. To further capture that dream life feeling, she brings little touches of favourite vacations to her everyday routine. Healthy treat meals such as tropical fruit for breakfast, taking an afternoon rest with a good book, and dressing in her nicest clothes are all small ways in which she can feel in vacation mode and thus, more relaxed, peaceful, and thankful.

26. **She has worked out what she truly values**, and uses these values to make the most of her life. She knows that hers will be different to others, so she doesn't base them on what friends or family show is important to them.

27. **She endeavours to listen more than she talks**, because she realises that if she is the one talking, she already knows all that stuff. But by listening to others she is more likely to learn something new. And, it's just good etiquette. People like you more when you are interested in them. Funny that!

28. **She has an elevated personal style**. She wears her nicer clothes even for everyday errands and outings. People commented at first ('Why so dressed up?') but now they know she is simply a woman who loves to dress well.

29. **She generates her desired feelings**. To feel cheerful and optimistic as her default, she practises these feelings daily. First she chooses them and then they become 'just how she is'.

30. **She believes in the power of her mind**. She knows that whatever she dreams of, she can have in her life. More health, beauty, increased earnings, a lovely home: she keeps these visions in mind and calls them to her with her beliefs. Everything ever invented began as an idea in

one person's mind. This thought gives her thrills!

31. **She doesn't mind getting older** because she knows *she is only getting better*, and the alternative is just too sad to think about. She enjoys the challenge of becoming fitter and healthier as she ages and knows that the best is yet to come!

32. **She is persistent**. No matter what, she continues on towards her goals. She knows that being persistent will take her far further than talent, skill, or even money. She knows that she will get there eventually, and she is willing to keep on putting one foot in front of the other.

33. **She makes the decision to attract, not chase**. Whether it is a love relationship, friendship, or in daily dealings with others, she is happy and calm. She no longer feels the need to impress people, rather, she shows she is *impressed by them*, which amazingly has the same effect!

34. **She surrounds herself with her favourite colours** by incorporating shades that make her feel happiest into her home décor, clothing and accessories, images she saves on Pinterest, stationery, makeup, and artwork at home. Doing this gives her a sense of contentment and

cohesiveness.

35. **She enjoys a simple life**. To not become overwhelmed, she has worked at simplifying every category in her life, even down to what she eats for dinner. Doing this gives her more energy since she is not having to deal with decision fatigue, which, when she heard of it realised was a real thing!

36. **She is clear on her goals**, yet flexible on how she is going to get there. She knows that she doesn't need to have all the answers, she just needs to focus on what she wants and head towards those things. She trusts that the path will appear as she steps forward.

37. **She retains her femininity**. Even though she loves to investigate side hustles, is a stout advocate of personal development, and is success-driven, she does so from a feminine state of enjoyment and ease. She keeps her masculine energy to a minimum, preferring instead to work in a relaxed and fluid manner.

38. **She looks after her body and mind**, by relaxing into the softness of her physical self, letting her shoulders drop, and remembering to breathe deeply. She calms her mind with soothing self-talk and chooses not to multi-task.

39. **She fuels herself well** by upgrading what she eats and drinks. She used to enjoy certain foods such as sweet treats, but she found that the more she chose different, healthier foods, the better she felt. And looked!

40. **She enjoys her love of beauty** unabashedly and takes delight in adding elegant touches to her home and herself.

41. **She is still herself.** She knows that by focusing on self-improvement, she doesn't need to be anyone other than who she already is. She is simply becoming the best version of herself and she loves that!

42. **She does things that are fun for her.** Being a chic success is not all about work, it's about play too, so she reads books that she enjoys, plays around with handcrafts, goes for walks in the sun, and meets friends for lunch or afternoon tea. She knows that balance is key.

43. **She dreams big** by conjuring up the most wonderful lifestyle she could imagine and works out how to make it happen. It's still a work in progress and might not be 'big' by others standards, but it's perfect for her.

44. **She motivates herself daily**. She knows that being a chic success doesn't come for free, so she combats laziness whenever it pops up. It just

doesn't feel satisfying to be slothful. Sometimes yes! But not all the time otherwise she'd never get anything done.

45. **She focuses on what is important**. She knows it's easier to 'major in the minor things', but success comes more when you do it the other way around. She makes sure she gets at least one or two important tasks done each day, and that way she knows she is always moving towards her goals.

46. **She plans little treats often**. Happiness comes when you always have something to look forward to, so she makes sure to include her favourite treats on a regular basis – a cozy novel to read, professional pedicure, lunch out, or a new lipstick. These things make her feel luxuriously pampered and they are worth the cost for her.

47. **She lives with integrity**, not only because it's the right thing to do, but because it makes her feel so good. Living life in accordance with her values and aspirations brings her the ultimate happiness.

48. **She is financially savvy,** choosing to live below her means, paying off all debt, learning about investments, buying consumer goods only after careful consideration, and looking around

for the best deal when she needs something. No purchase is worth the stress for her – she learned that lesson when she was younger!

49. **She is open to new ideas** and ways to improve her health, happiness, and relationships. She reads articles online and picks up the latest books on self-development for a shot of inspiration and encouragement.

50. **She is determined to make her life a wonderful creation**, by the way she dresses, keeps her home, does her work, comports herself, in her interactions with others, and how she spends her time. *She endeavours to always show up as the ideal version of herself.*

Isn't 'she' fabulous? And also, 'she' can be you, or your own idealistic version of you. And me. And everyone else if they wish. Take her on for yourself and know that you can step into your new 'reality' any time you like.

As you read and digest this book, focus on the ideal version of yourself and how *you* want to show up. Practice new ways of being. Build on your success habits and watch the vision of your dream life start to fall into place. You could be living a lifestyle each day that is aligning with the person you've always wanted to be.

It works! It really does work! And *you* get to benefit. Good luck. I know you can do it. Have fun!

To Finish

Thank you for reading *100 Ways to be a Chic Success and Create Your Dream Life*.

I sincerely hope you gained inspiration from these pages as well as encouragement to design your most wonderful daily experience and enjoy living it.

If you have a moment, I would be beyond grateful if you could leave me a review on Amazon. Even a few words are perfect – you don't have to write a lot. A review is the best compliment you can give to an author. It helps others like yourself find my books, and I'd love to get my message of living well through an inspired mindset to as many ladies as possible.

And if you have a friend who you think would enjoy this book, please tell them about it, or loan them your copy. Did you know that most libraries welcome suggestions on what to purchase? Maybe you might like to suggest this book for your local public library. That way, lots more people can read it!

If you have anything you'd like to say to me personally, please feel free to write:

fiona@howtobechic.com

Maybe you have a book idea for me, want to let me know what you thought of this book, or have even spotted an error. I hope not, but if you do find a typo, please let me know!

Think of me as your friend all the way down in New Zealand, cheering you on and wishing you well. You can add as many fun and fabulous details as you like into your daily life. No-one else gets to have an opinion on any of this except for you. Why *not* live a life filled with every delight you could ever imagine? That's what it feels like when you decide to become a chic success and create *your* dream life.

With all my best to you, and I look forward to seeing you in my next book!

Fiona

100 Ways to be a Chic Success and Create Your Dream Life

About the Author

Fiona Ferris lives in the beautiful and sunny wine region of Hawke's Bay, New Zealand, with her husband, Paul, their rescue cat Nina, rescue dogs Daphne and Chloe, and their cousin Micky dog.

She loves to write about living a fabulous life, chic self-development and cultivating a feminine personal style. Fiona is passionate about the topic of living well, in particular that a simple and beautiful life can be achieved without spending a lot of money

Her books are published in five languages currently: English, Spanish, Russian, Lithuanian and Vietnamese. She also runs an online home study program for aspiring non-fiction authors.

To learn more about Fiona, you can connect with her at:
howtobechic.com
fionaferris.com
facebook.com/fionaferrisauthor
twitter.com/fiona_ferris
instagram.com/fionaferrisnz
youtube.com/fionaferris

Fiona's other books are listed on the next page, and you can also find them at:
amazon.com/author/fionaferris

FIONA FERRIS

Other books by Fiona Ferris

Thirty Chic Days: *Practical inspiration for a beautiful life*

Thirty More Chic Days: *Creating an inspired mindset for a magical life*

Thirty Chic Days Vol. 3: *Nurturing a happy relationship, staying youthful, being your best self, and having a ton of fun at the same time*

Thirty Slim Days: *Create your slender and healthy life in a fun and enjoyable way*

Financially Chic: *Live a luxurious life on a budget, learn to love managing money, and grow your wealth*

How to be Chic in the Winter: *Living slim, happy and stylish during the cold season*

How to be Chic in the Summer: *Living well, keeping your cool and dressing stylishly when it's warm outside*

A Chic and Simple Christmas: *Celebrate the holiday season with ease and grace*

The Original 30 Chic Days Blog Series: *Be inspired by the online series that started it all*

30 Chic Days at Home: *Self-care tips for when you have to stay at home, or any other time when life is challenging*

30 Chic Days at Home Vol. 2: *Creating a serene spa-like ambience in your home for soothing peace and relaxation*

The Chic Author*: Create your dream career and lifestyle, writing and self-publishing non-fiction books*

The Chic Closet*: Inspired ideas to develop your personal style, fall in love with your wardrobe, and bring back the joy in dressing yourself*

The Peaceful Life*: Slowing down, choosing happiness, nurturing your feminine self, and finding sanctuary in your home*

Loving Your Epic Small Life*: Thriving in your own style, being happy at home, and the art of exquisite self-care*

The Glam Life*: Uplevel everything in a fun way using glamour as your filter to the world*

100 Ways *to Live a Luxurious Life on a Budget*

100 Ways *to Declutter Your Home*

100 Ways *to Live a European Inspired Life*

100 Ways *to Enjoy Self-Care for Gentle Wellbeing and a Healthy Body Image*

100 Ways *to be That Girl*

Printed in Great Britain
by Amazon

37351830R00057